DIVINE ENCOUNTERS

Discovering the Depth and Power of God's Names

DAMIANO B. CENTOLA

Trilogy Christian Publishers
A Wholly Owned Subsidiary of Trinity Broadcasting Network
2442 Michelle Drive
Tustin, CA 92780
Copyright © 2025 by Bryan'Damiano A.B. Centola
Scripture quotations are taken from the Amplified® Bible, Classic Edition (AMPC), Copyright © 2015 by The Lockman Foundation. Used by permission. www.Lockman.org.

All rights reserved, including the right to reproduce this book or portions thereof in any form whatsoever.
For information, address Trilogy Christian Publishing
Rights Department, 2442 Michelle Drive, Tustin, CA 92780.
Trilogy Christian Publishing/ TBN and colophon are trademarks of Trinity Broadcasting Network.
For information about special discounts for bulk purchases, please contact Trilogy Christian Publishing.
Trilogy Disclaimer: The views and content expressed in this book are those of the author and may not necessarily reflect the views and doctrine of Trilogy Christian Publishing or the Trinity Broadcasting Network.

10 9 8 7 6 5 4 3 2 1
Library of Congress Cataloging-in-Publication Data is available.
ISBN 979-8-89597-260-1
ISBN (ebook) 979-8-89597-261-8

TABLE OF CONTENTS

Introduction........................9

1 - YHWH
(Yahweh)........................11

2 - Adonai
(Lord) 17

3 - Elohim
(God)...........................25

4 - El Shaddai
(God Almighty)..................33

5 - El Elyon
(Most High God).................39

6 - Jehovah Jireh
(The Lord Will Provide) 45

7 - Jehovah Rapha
(The Lord Who Heals) 51

8 - Jehovah Nissi
(The Lord Is My Banner) 59

9 - Jehovah Shalom
(The Lord Is Peace). 65

10 - Jehovah Tsidkenu
(The Lord Our Righteousness) 71

11 - Jehovah Shammah
(The Lord Is There). 77

12 - Emmanuel
(God with Us) 83

13 - Yahweh Yireh
(The Lord Will Provide) 89

14 - Jehovah Rohi
(The Lord Is My Shepherd) 95

15 - El Roi
(The God Who Sees). 101

16 - Jehovah Mekoddishkem (The Lord
Who Sanctifies You) 107

17 - El Olam
(The Everlasting God)..............113

18 - Jehovah Sabaoth
(The Lord of Hosts) 119

19 - The Rock 125

20 - The Word 131

21 - The Holy One of Israel 137

22 - The Lion of the Tribe of Judah ...143

23 - The Ancient of Days 149

24 - Ehyeh Asher Ehyeh 155

Conclusion 161

INTRODUCTION

The names of the Lord reveal His character, His nature, and His relationship with us. Each name is a reflection of His divine attributes—His power, His faithfulness, His provision, and His nearness. When we explore and understand these names, we deepen our worship, for we are not just calling upon a distant God, but intimately connecting with who He is. Knowing His names allows us to approach Him with reverence, trust, and expectation, as each name carries a promise, a truth, and a reminder of His unchanging nature. Whether we cry out to Him as Jehovah-Jireh, our Provider, or as El Shaddai, the Almighty God, His names anchor us in His love, strengthen our faith, and transform our understanding of Him.

1
YHWH
(YAHWEH)

Hebrew: יְהֹוָה (YHWH or Yahweh)
Greek: Κύριος (Kyrios) – the Septuagint (Greek Old Testament) often translates YHWH as "Kyrios" (Lord)
English: LORD (in most English Bibles, it is written in all capitals)

SCRIPTURAL REFERENCE:

"God said to Moses, 'I AM WHO I AM.' And He said, 'Say this to the people of Israel: I AM has sent me to you.'"

Exodus 3:14

Genesis 2:4, Isaiah 42:8, Deuteronomy 6:4

Hebrew: The name YHWH (יהוה), often vocalized as Yahweh, is derived from the Hebrew verb "to be" (היה, hayah), and it is often interpreted as "He Who Is," or "I AM WHO I AM." This name points to God's eternal, self-existing nature—He exists outside of time, and His being is uncaused and independent.

Greek: The Septuagint (Greek Old Testament) uses "Κύριος" (Kyrios), meaning Lord, to translate YHWH. While this doesn't capture the full depth of the Hebrew name, it emphasizes God's sovereign rulership.

English: Most English Bibles translate YHWH as LORD (in all caps) to signify its uniqueness as God's personal name.

YHWH (YAHWEH)

TIME OF AGE:

Biblical Context:

YHWH first appears in Genesis 2:4 in relation to the creation account, where it highlights God's personal involvement with humanity. However, its full revelation came when God spoke to Moses in Exodus 3, identifying Himself as the "I AM" to the Israelites. This was a pivotal moment in biblical history because it established God's covenant name with His chosen people during the period of the Exodus (around 15th-13th century BC). Historical Context: In ancient times, names held deep significance, revealing something essential about the nature or role of a person. YHWH, with its connection to the verb "to be," emphasizes that God is eternal and sovereign. He is not bound by time or space and is the source of all life and existence. This name was especially meaningful to the Israelites as they were about to witness God's power in delivering them from Egypt.

Theological Significance:

YHWH is the name that speaks to God's faithfulness in His covenant relationship with Israel. It signifies not just His power but also His personal, intimate care for His people. Unlike other nations' gods, YHWH is relational and actively involved in the lives of His followers.

For Believers Today:

The name Yahweh reminds us of God's unchanging and eternal nature. Just as He was with the Israelites, He is present with us. He is the "I AM" in our lives, constant and faithful in every season, independent of circumstances. Understanding Yahweh as the self-existent One encourages believers to trust in His sovereignty, especially in times of uncertainty.

YHWH (YAHWEH)

PRAYER

YHWH, our Eternal God,

We come before You with reverence and awe, acknowledging Your greatness and sovereignty over all creation. You are the One who was, who is, and who is to come—the Alpha and Omega. Thank You for revealing Yourself to us through Your name, reminding us of Your faithfulness, love, and presence in our lives. Lord, help us to live in a way that honors Your name, reflecting Your character in our thoughts, words, and actions. Teach us to trust in Your plans, knowing that You are always working for our good. May we seek You earnestly and draw closer to You, finding strength and peace in Your eternal truth. As we navigate the challenges of life, may Your name be our refuge and strength. We pray for guidance, wisdom, and discernment in all our endeavors. Help us to be ambassadors of Your love and grace, sharing the hope we have in You with those around us. Thank You, YHWH, for being our Creator, Sustainer, and Redeemer. We honor and worship You today and always. In the powerful name of Jesus, we pray. Amen.

2
ADONAI
(LORD)

Hebrew: אֲדֹנָי (Adonai)
Greek: Κύριος (Kyrios)
English: Lord

SCRIPTURAL REFERENCE:

"But Abram said, 'O Lord GOD, what will you give me, for I continue childless...?'"

Genesis 15:2

Psalm 8:1, Isaiah 6:1, Ezekiel 16:8

Hebrew: Adonai comes from the root word "adon" (אָדוֹן), meaning "lord" or "master." It is a plural form used as a respectful and reverential way to address God, emphasizing His supreme authority and lordship over all creation. The plural form conveys majesty and honor, acknowledging God as Master of all.

Greek: The Greek word Kyrios (Κύριος) in the Septuagint also translates to "Lord" or "Master," mirroring the Hebrew meaning and usage. It conveys the authority of God over His people and creation.

English: In most English translations, Adonai is rendered as "Lord" (capitalized but not in all caps), distinguishing it from "YHWH" (rendered as LORD in all caps).

ADONAI (LORD)

TIME OF AGE:

Biblical Context:

The name Adonai is used throughout the Old Testament as a title of respect and reverence. In Genesis 15:2, Abraham addresses God as Adonai while recognizing His sovereign authority over his life and the fulfillment of God's promises. It was especially important in contexts where God's role as a ruler and guide is being emphasized. It came to be used more frequently by the Israelites in later biblical periods as they grew cautious about pronouncing the name YHWH out of reverence and fear of misusing it. Historical Context: During ancient times, addressing someone as "lord" (adon) was a common way of showing respect, especially toward a king, master, or ruler. By using the title Adonai for God, the Israelites acknowledged His ultimate rulership and authority over their lives. This was particularly important in cultures with polytheistic beliefs, where multiple gods were worshipped—calling God Adonai emphasized His unique sovereignty above all other so-called gods and earthly rulers.

Theological Significance:
Adonai conveys God's lordship and mastery over all creation. It reminds believers that God is not only the Creator but also the sovereign King who governs everything. He has the authority to guide, command, and direct the lives of His people. This term also highlights the relationship between God and His people: God as the Master and His people as servants who submit to His will.

For Believers Today:

Understanding God as Adonai helps believers recognize the authority and power God holds over their lives. He is not just a distant figure but the personal Lord

ADONAI (LORD)

who directs and guides. In submitting to Him as Adonai, we acknowledge His rightful rule and trust in His leadership, knowing that His plans and purposes are for our good. Recognizing God as Adonai also calls for obedience and submission, as He is not only Savior but also the Master who deserves our reverence and complete surrender.

DIVINE ENCOUNTERS

PRAYER

Adonai,

We come before You in reverence, recognizing You as our Lord and Master. Thank You for Your constant presence in our lives and for Your authority over all creation. We acknowledge Your sovereignty and the power of Your Word, which brings life and order to our world. As we seek to honor You as our Adonai, help us to submit to Your will and to follow Your guidance in every aspect of our lives. Teach us to listen for Your voice and to respond with obedience, trusting that Your plans are good and perfect. May we reflect Your love and grace in our interactions with others, serving as instruments of Your peace and compassion. Strengthen us to stand firm in faith and to boldly proclaim Your truth in a world that desperately needs to know You. Thank You for being

ADONAI (LORD)

our Lord, our refuge, and our strength. We surrender our hearts to You and ask for Your wisdom to navigate life's challenges. In the name of Jesus, our Savior, we pray. Amen.

3
ELOHIM
(GOD)

Hebrew: אֱלֹהִים (Elohim)
Greek: Θεός (Theos)
English: God

SCRIPTURAL REFERENCE:

"In the beginning, God (Elohim) created the heavens and the earth."
Genesis 1:1

Deuteronomy 6:4, Psalm 19:1, Isaiah 40:28

Hebrew: Elohim is a plural noun but often takes a singular meaning when referring to the one true God. The plural form conveys majesty, fullness, and the idea of the divine nature encompassing all power, might, and authority. It emphasizes God as the Creator and Sustainer of everything.

Greek: In the New Testament and the Septuagint (Greek Old Testament), Theos (Θεός) is the equivalent of Elohim, meaning "God." It refers to the supreme divine being, emphasizing His nature as the all-powerful Creator and ruler.

English: Translated as "God" in English, Elohim underscores God's sovereign role in creation and His omnipotence.

ELOHIM (GOD)

TIME OF AGE:

Biblical Context:

The name Elohim is introduced in the very first verse of the Bible, establishing God as the Creator of the universe. This sets the stage for His relationship with humanity and the entire creation. Elohim is used over 2,500 times in the Old Testament, particularly in contexts related to God's power, sovereignty, and divine nature. Historical Context: In the ancient Near Eastern context, the word elohim could refer to divine beings or gods in a general sense. However, when applied to the God of Israel, Elohim takes on a singular meaning, emphasizing His supremacy over all other "gods." While neighboring cultures worshiped multiple deities, Israel's use of Elohim asserted that the one true God was the Creator of all things. This distinction was crucial during the time when Israel was surrounded by polytheistic cultures.

Theological Significance:

Elohim highlights God's transcendence, power, and majesty. It affirms that God is above and beyond His creation, yet He is also intimately involved with it. This name also subtly points to the complexity of God's nature, as seen in the plural form, which some theologians see as an early hint of the Trinity (Father, Son, and Holy Spirit) without explicitly defining it.

For Believers Today:

Recognizing God as Elohim encourages believers to view God as the ultimate Creator and Sustainer of all life. It reminds us of His power and control over the universe, and at the same time, His personal involvement in our lives. In worship, we can honor Him as the Creator who formed the heavens and the earth and trust that the same power that created the universe is at work in our lives. It also fosters a sense of awe, reverence, and humility, knowing that we are part of His creation and subject to His divine will.

DIVINE ENCOUNTERS

PRAYER

Elohim, Creator of the heavens and the earth, We come before You in awe of Your infinite power and majesty. You are the One who spoke the universe into existence, who crafted every detail of creation with purpose and beauty. Thank You for being our strong and mighty God, who holds all things together and governs the cosmos with Your wisdom. As we reflect on Your nature as Elohim, remind us of Your authority in our lives. Help us to trust in Your perfect plan and to lean on Your strength in our moments of weakness. May we recognize Your hand in our lives and the world around us, acknowledging that every good gift comes from You. We pray for a deeper understanding of Your creation and our role within it. Inspire us to be good stewards of the gifts You have given us, and help us to reflect Your image in our actions

ELOHIM (GOD)

and decisions. In the name of Jesus, our Creator and Redeemer, we pray. Amen.

4
EL SHADDAI
(GOD ALMIGHTY)

Hebrew: אֵל שַׁדַּי (El Shaddai)
Greek: Παντοκράτωρ Θεός (Pantokrator Theos) – meaning "Almighty God"
English: God Almighty

SCRIPTURAL REFERENCE:

"When Abram was ninety-nine years old, the LORD appeared to Abram and said to him, 'I am God Almighty (El Shaddai); walk before me, and be blameless.'"

Genesis 17:1

Genesis 28:3, Psalm 91:1, Job 5:17

Hebrew: El Shaddai is often translated as "God Almighty." The word El means "God," and Shaddai is commonly understood as "Almighty" or "All-Sufficient." Some scholars suggest that Shaddai may also come from a root meaning "mountain," symbolizing strength and immovability. This name emphasizes God's overwhelming power and sufficiency to provide for His people.

Greek: In the Septuagint, El Shaddai is rendered as Pantokrator, meaning "Almighty" or "All-Powerful," further emphasizing God's unmatched power and sovereignty.

English: Translated as "God Almighty" in most English versions, El Shaddai highlights God's omnipotence and His ability to fulfill His promises.

EL SHADDAI (GOD ALMIGHTY)

TIME OF AGE:

Biblical Context:

The name El Shaddai is first used in Genesis 17:1 when God reaffirms His covenant with Abraham and promises to multiply his descendants. This was a time when Abraham needed assurance of God's power to bring about what seemed impossible—descendants through a wife who was barren. The name underscores God's ability to do the impossible and provide abundantly for His people. It is used frequently in the patriarchal narratives and in the book of Job to emphasize God's power and sufficiency in times of trial. Historical Context: In ancient times, El Shaddai would have been a comforting name for the early Israelites, who were surrounded by nations with multiple gods. They could trust that El Shaddai, their God, was more powerful than any other force in the world. The name was particularly significant during periods of struggle or uncertainty, such as Abraham's journey of faith, the wanderings of Israel, or Job's intense suffering. It affirmed that God had the power to control all events and that nothing was too difficult for Him.

Theological Significance:

El Shaddai reveals the nature of God as both powerful and nurturing. While He is omnipotent, able to do all things, the name also suggests His sufficiency to meet the needs of His people. He is not only strong but also the source of blessing, provision, and care. The use of this name demonstrates God's commitment to His covenant and the assurance that He will fulfill His promises.

For Believers Today:

Knowing God as El Shaddai reassures believers of His power and provision in

EL SHADDAI (GOD ALMIGHTY)

all circumstances. Just as He was able to make a barren woman bear children or to sustain Job through his suffering, He is able to meet us in our times of need. El Shaddai reminds us that God is more than enough—He is sufficient to provide for our physical, emotional, and spiritual needs. This name inspires trust in His ability to do the impossible and encourages us to depend on His strength rather than our own.

DIVINE ENCOUNTERS

PRAYER

El Shaddai, All-Sufficient One,

We come before You with hearts full of gratitude for Your abundant provision and care. Thank You for being our source of strength, comfort, and sustenance. In times of need, remind us that You are more than enough to meet our every requirement. Help us to trust in Your sufficiency, knowing that You are capable of providing for our physical, emotional, and spiritual needs. When we face challenges, may we lean on Your everlasting arms and find peace in Your presence. Guide us to reflect Your generosity and compassion to others, sharing the blessings we have received from You. As we walk through life's journey, may we always remember that in You, we lack nothing. We declare our faith in You, El Shaddai, and thank You for Your unwavering love and faithfulness. In Jesus' name, we pray. Amen.

5
EL ELYON
(MOST HIGH GOD)

Hebrew: אֵל עֶלְיוֹן (El Elyon)
Greek: ὁ Θεὸς ὁ ὕψιστος (ho Theos ho Hypsistos)
English: Most High God

SCRIPTURAL REFERENCE:

"And Melchizedek king of Salem brought out bread and wine. He was priest of God Most High (El Elyon)."

Genesis 14:18

Psalm 7:17, Psalm 57:2, Daniel 4:34

Hebrew: El Elyon means "God Most High." El refers to God, and Elyon comes from a root word meaning "to go up" or "to ascend," signifying God's supremacy, exalted position, and authority over all things. It emphasizes God's position as the highest, above all gods and powers.

Greek: The Septuagint translates El Elyon as "ὁ Θεὸς ὁ ὕψιστος" (ho Theos ho Hypsistos), meaning "the Most High God," emphasizing the same concept of God's ultimate sovereignty and rule over everything.

English: Translated as "Most High God" or simply "God Most High" in English, this name stresses God's unparalleled status and authority.

EL ELYON (MOST HIGH GOD)

TIME OF AGE:

Biblical Context:

El Elyon first appears in Genesis 14:18 when Melchizedek, the king and priest of Salem, blesses Abram in the name of God Most High. This encounter underscores God's role as sovereign over all nations and peoples, including those outside of the immediate covenant community (such as Melchizedek's kingdom of Salem). In Psalm 57:2, David cries out to El Elyon in times of trouble, recognizing God's supreme authority to protect and deliver him.

Historical Context:

In the ancient Near Eastern world, many cultures worshipped multiple gods, with different gods assigned to various aspects of life and nature. The Israelites, however, worshiped El Elyon, the God

Most High, affirming that their God was not just one among many, but the supreme ruler over all. The use of El Elyon set Yahweh apart as the God above all so-called gods, whether spiritual beings or earthly rulers. This name would have been particularly significant in a polytheistic context, emphasizing monotheism and God's ultimate power over all creation.

Theological Significance:

El Elyon highlights God's sovereignty, authority, and transcendence. It affirms that God is exalted above all other powers, rulers, and forces in the universe. This name reflects the truth that God is the ruler over all creation, and no force can rival His majesty. It also assures believers that God is supreme over all circumstances, no matter how powerful other entities or situations may seem.

EL ELYON (MOST HIGH GOD)

For Believers Today:

Understanding God as El Elyon brings comfort and peace in recognizing that God is in control of everything. There is no power, authority, or situation greater than Him. In times of uncertainty, fear, or conflict, believers can trust that El Elyon is above it all, and His plans cannot be thwarted. This name reminds us of God's sovereignty and gives us confidence that He reigns over every aspect of our lives and the world at large.

DIVINE ENCOUNTERS

PRAYER

Most High God, El Elyon,

We come before You in reverence, acknowledging Your supreme authority and sovereignty over all creation. You are exalted above the heavens and the earth, and we recognize Your majesty and power. Thank You for being our refuge and source of strength. Help us to trust in Your higher ways and to seek Your guidance in all aspects of our lives. May we honor You in our thoughts, words, and actions, reflecting Your greatness to those around us. As we face challenges, remind us that You are in control and that nothing is too difficult for You. We praise You for Your love and mercy, and we rest in the assurance that You are always with us. In Jesus' name, we pray. Amen.

6
JEHOVAH JIREH
(THE LORD WILL PROVIDE)

Hebrew: יְהוָה יִרְאֶה (YHWH Yireh)
Greek: ὁ Κύριος ὁ ὁρῶν (ho Kyrios ho horon) – meaning "The Lord who sees" or "The Lord who provides"
English: The Lord Will Provide

SCRIPTURAL REFERENCE:

"So Abraham called the name of that place, 'The LORD will provide' (Jehovah Jireh), as it is said to this day, 'On the mount of the LORD it shall be provided.'"

Genesis 22:14

DIVINE ENCOUNTERS

Psalm 23:1, Philippians 4:19

Hebrew: Jehovah Jireh comes from the Hebrew phrase "YHWH Yireh," which means "The LORD will provide" or "The LORD will see to it." The root word Yireh (יִרְאֶה) is related to seeing, which in this context conveys the idea that God foresees our needs and provides for them at the right time.

Greek: The Septuagint uses "ὁ Κύριος ὁ ὁρῶν" (ho Kyrios ho horon), meaning "The Lord who sees" or "provides," capturing the idea of God's provision through His foresight.

English: Translated as "The Lord Will Provide," it conveys God's ability to meet the needs of His people through His divine foresight and care.

JEHOVAH JIREH (THE LORD WILL PROVIDE)

TIME OF AGE:

Biblical Context:

Jehovah Jireh is first used in Genesis 22:14, after God provides a ram for Abraham to sacrifice in place of his son Isaac. This name of God was revealed in a moment of great faith and obedience, when Abraham demonstrated his trust in God's provision. The ram provided in Isaac's place symbolized God's ultimate provision, pointing to His future provision of salvation through Jesus Christ.

Historical Context:

In the ancient world, provision and sustenance were seen as marks of favor from the gods. For Israel, this name set Yahweh apart as the one true God who personally provides for His people. It would have resonated deeply with a people who were often nomadic or lived in a land where survival depended on divine provision for their crops, flocks, and safety. Jehovah Jireh reminded them that their sustenance did not come from pagan rituals or chance but from the Lord who sees and provides.

Theological Significance:

The name Jehovah Jireh reveals God's intimate knowledge of our needs and His ability to meet them, often in unexpected ways. It reflects God's faithfulness to His promises and His grace in providing not just material needs but also spiritual sustenance and salvation. This name assures believers that God sees their needs and provides at the right time, in His perfect wisdom.

Application:

For Believers Today: Jehovah Jireh is a powerful reminder that God knows our needs and provides for us in ways we

JEHOVAH JIREH (THE LORD WILL PROVIDE)

might not always expect. Whether we are in need of physical resources, spiritual renewal, or emotional support, we can trust that God will see to it and meet those needs. This name encourages us to have faith like Abraham, trusting that God will always provide—even when we don't see how it will happen. It also challenges us to recognize God's past provisions in our lives and give thanks, knowing He is the same God who will continue to care for us.

DIVINE ENCOUNTERS

PRAYER

Jehovah Jireh,

Thank You for being our provider and for meeting our needs according to Your riches in glory. We are grateful for the ways You have shown Your faithfulness in our lives. Help us to trust in Your provision, even when circumstances seem uncertain. May we recognize Your hand in both the abundance and the challenges, knowing that You are always working for our good. Teach us to seek You first and to rely on Your wisdom as we navigate our daily lives. As we reflect on Your name, may we become vessels of Your provision, sharing generously with others as You have generously provided for us. We thank You for Your unending grace and love. In Jesus' name, we pray. Amen.

7
JEHOVAH RAPHA
(THE LORD WHO HEALS)

Hebrew: יְהוָה רֹפְאֶךָ (YHWH Ropheka)
Greek: Κύριος ὁ ἰατρός (Kyrios ho Iatros)
– meaning "The Lord the Healer"
English: The Lord Who Heals

SCRIPTURAL REFERENCE:

"For I am the LORD who heals you (Jehovah Rapha)."

Exodus 15:26

Psalm 103:2-3, Jeremiah 30:17, Matthew 9:35

Hebrew: Jehovah Rapha means "The Lord Who Heals." The Hebrew word Rapha (רֹפֵא) comes from a root meaning "to heal," "to restore," or "to make whole." This name emphasizes God's power to bring physical, emotional, and spiritual healing.

Greek: In the Greek, Kyrios ho Iatros translates to "The Lord the Healer," emphasizing God's role as the physician who can restore health and wholeness.

English: Translated as "The Lord Who Heals," this name highlights God's ability to heal all forms of sickness, brokenness, and disease, both of the body and the soul.

JEHOVAH RAPHA (THE LORD WHO HEALS)

TIME OF AGE:

Biblical Context:

The name Jehovah Rapha is revealed in Exodus 15:26, after God had healed the bitter waters of Marah for the Israelites during their journey in the wilderness. God promised to keep them from the diseases that afflicted Egypt if they remained faithful to Him. This demonstrated God's concern not only for their spiritual obedience but also for their physical well-being. Throughout the Old Testament, God is often referred to as the healer of His people, whether from disease, spiritual ailments, or societal brokenness.

Historical Context:

In the ancient world, illness was often seen as a curse or punishment from the gods. Israel's understanding of Jehovah Rapha set Yahweh apart as a God who not only had the power to heal but also had compassion for His people. This was especially important during times of plague, illness, and personal affliction, as it established God as the ultimate source of healing rather than relying on superstitions or pagan rituals.

Theological Significance:

Jehovah Rapha reveals God's nature as the source of all healing—physically, emotionally, and spiritually. The name underscores that God cares deeply about the wholeness and well-being of His people. It also points toward the ultimate healing found in the redemptive work of Jesus Christ, who heals not only diseases but also the deeper wounds of sin and death. God's healing is complete, encompassing all dimensions of life.

For Believers Today:

Jehovah Rapha offers comfort and hope

JEHOVAH RAPHA (THE LORD WHO HEALS)

for those in need of healing, whether from physical illness, emotional wounds, or spiritual brokenness. It reminds us to turn to God in faith, trusting that He is both willing and able to heal us according to His perfect will. While we may not always understand how or when healing comes, we can rest in the assurance that God is at work, restoring us to wholeness. This name encourages us to seek God as our ultimate physician and to trust Him for healing in every area of life.

DIVINE ENCOUNTERS

PRAYER

Jehovah Rapha, our Healer,

We come before You with grateful hearts, acknowledging Your power to heal and restore. We thank You for the promise of healing found in Your Word, and we trust in Your ability to mend not only our physical bodies but also our emotional and spiritual wounds. Lord, we lift up those who are suffering, whether from illness, pain, or despair. May Your healing touch be upon them, bringing comfort and restoration. We pray for wisdom for healthcare providers and strength for caregivers. Help us to remember that healing is not just a physical restoration but a deep, holistic process that encompasses body, mind, and spirit. Teach us to lean on You in times of distress and to seek Your presence as our ultimate source of hope. Thank You, Jehovah Rapha, for Your unfailing love

JEHOVAH RAPHA (THE LORD WHO HEALS)

and compassion. May we always look to You for our healing and strength, knowing that in You, we find wholeness and peace. In Jesus' name, we pray. Amen.

8
JEHOVAH NISSI
(THE LORD IS MY BANNER)

Hebrew: יְהוָה נִסִּי (YHWH Nissi)
Greek: Κύριος τὸ σημεῖόν μου (Kyrios to Semeion mou) – meaning "The Lord my sign" or "The Lord my banner"
English: The Lord Is My Banner

SCRIPTURAL REFERENCE:

"And Moses built an altar and called the name of it, 'The LORD is my banner' (Jehovah Nissi)."

Exodus 17:15

Psalm 60:4, Isaiah 11:10-12

Hebrew: Jehovah Nissi means "The Lord is My Banner." The word Nissi (נִסִּי) comes from Nes (נֵס), meaning a banner, standard, or ensign. A banner was often used as a rallying point during battle, symbolizing victory, protection, and a visible sign of God's presence.

Greek: The Greek translation to Semeion mou refers to "a sign" or "standard" that would signify God's presence and help in battle.

English: In English, "The Lord Is My Banner" conveys the image of God as the standard-bearer in times of conflict, under whose protection and guidance His people march and find victory.

JEHOVAH NISSI (THE LORD IS MY BANNER)

TIME OF AGE:

Biblical Context:

Jehovah Nissi is revealed in Exodus 17 after the Israelites' victory over the Amalekites. During the battle, as long as Moses kept his hands raised (a symbol of reliance on God), the Israelites were winning. After the battle, Moses built an altar to commemorate God's victory and named it Jehovah Nissi, acknowledging that the Lord was their banner of victory. This was a reminder that it was God's power that gave them victory, not their own strength.

Historical Context:

In ancient warfare, a banner or standard was a crucial symbol around which troops would rally. It was a sign of leadership, unity, and protection. By calling God Jehovah Nissi, the Israelites were declaring that God Himself was their rallying point and the source of their strength in battle. This name would have been especially significant during Israel's many conflicts with surrounding nations, affirming that their trust was not in human strength but in the Lord's power.

Theological Significance:

Jehovah Nissi signifies God's role as the protector and deliverer of His people. The name implies that God goes before His people in battle, ensuring their victory when they rely on Him. It reflects the idea of God's people uniting under His authority and finding strength in His presence. In a broader spiritual sense, it points to God as the ultimate victor over evil and chaos, and His banner is one of peace, truth, and salvation.

For Believers Today:

Jehovah Nissi encourages believers to

JEHOVAH NISSI (THE LORD IS MY BANNER)

look to God as their source of victory in all aspects of life, especially during times of spiritual warfare, challenges, or difficulties. Just as the Israelites rallied under God's banner in battle, we can rally under His protection, trusting that He fights for us and leads us to triumph. The name also reminds us that our identity and unity as God's people come from rallying around His truth, His Word, and His presence. It encourages us to declare God as our banner, lifting Him high in our lives as a testimony of His power and grace.

DIVINE ENCOUNTERS

PRAYER FOR JEHOVAH NISSI

Jehovah Nissi, our Banner,

We come before You with grateful hearts, acknowledging Your mighty power and protection in our lives. Thank You for being our refuge and strength, our source of victory in times of battle. Help us to remember that, with You as our banner, we are never alone in our struggles. Grant us the courage to face our challenges, knowing that You fight for us and lead us to triumph. May we lift high Your banner in our lives, proclaiming Your faithfulness and love to the world around us. Strengthen our faith and help us to trust in Your guidance, recognizing that our victory comes from You alone. In the mighty name of Jesus, we pray. Amen.

9
JEHOVAH SHALOM
(THE LORD IS PEACE)

Hebrew: יְהוָה שָׁלוֹם (YHWH Shalom)
Greek: Κύριος ἡ εἰρήνη (Kyrios hē eirēnē) – meaning "The Lord is peace"
English: The Lord Is Peace

SCRIPTURAL REFERENCE:

"Then Gideon built an altar there to the LORD and called it, 'The LORD is Peace' (Jehovah Shalom). To this day it stands at Ophrah, which belongs to the Abiezrites."

Judges 6:24

Isaiah 9:6, Philippians 4:7

Hebrew: Jehovah Shalom translates to "The Lord is Peace." The term Shalom (שָׁלוֹם) encompasses a broad range of meanings, including peace, completeness, welfare, and wholeness. It signifies not just the absence of conflict but also the presence of well-being and harmony in all aspects of life.

Greek: The Greek translation hē eirēnē refers specifically to peace, indicating tranquility and wholeness.

English: In English, The Lord Is Peace captures the essence of God as the source of true and lasting peace in our lives.

JEHOVAH SHALOM (THE LORD IS PEACE)

TIME OF AGE:

Biblical Context:

The name Jehovah Shalom is first used in Judges 6:24 after Gideon encounters the angel of the Lord and receives assurance that he will not die after seeing the angel. Gideon builds an altar to honor God and names it Jehovah Shalom, recognizing that God provides peace amid fear and uncertainty. This name is particularly relevant in the context of Israel's cycles of turmoil and conflict during the time of the judges.

Historical Context:

In the ancient world, peace was often viewed as a divine blessing and a desired state in personal and communal life. The Israelites faced constant threats from surrounding nations, making the assurance of peace from God vital for their survival and stability. By naming God Jehovah Shalom, Gideon acknowledged that true peace comes from a relationship with the Lord, rather than merely the absence of external conflict.

Theological Significance:

Jehovah Shalom highlights God's role as the giver of peace, both internally and externally. It emphasizes that peace is a fundamental aspect of God's nature and His relationship with His people. The name points to the promise of a Messiah who would ultimately bring peace, as prophesied in Isaiah 9:6, where Jesus is referred to as the "Prince of Peace." This name assures believers that true peace is found in God alone, regardless of circumstances.

For Believers Today:

Jehovah Shalom offers hope and comfort in a world often filled with turmoil and

JEHOVAH SHALOM (THE LORD IS PEACE)

unrest. It reminds believers that true peace is not found in circumstances or worldly solutions but in a relationship with God. In times of anxiety, stress, or conflict, we can turn to Jehovah Shalom and find reassurance and rest in His presence. This name encourages us to seek peace with God and among ourselves, reflecting the peace we receive from Him in our relationships and communities.

DIVINE ENCOUNTERS

PRAYER

Jehovah Shalom,

We come before You, acknowledging You as Jehovah Shalom, the God of peace. In a world filled with chaos and uncertainty, we seek Your perfect peace that surpasses all understanding. Calm our anxious hearts and quiet our restless minds as we rest in Your presence. Help us to experience Your peace in every situation we face, reminding us that You are our refuge and strength. May Your peace guard our hearts and minds, bringing clarity and assurance in times of trouble. As we reflect Your peace in our lives, empower us to be instruments of peace to others. Let us spread Your love and tranquility wherever we go. Thank You for being our source of peace, and may we always find comfort in You. In Jesus' name, we pray. Amen.

10
JEHOVAH TSIDKENU
(THE LORD OUR RIGHTEOUSNESS)

Hebrew: יְהוָה צִדְקֵנוּ (YHWH Tsidkenu)
Greek: Κύριος ἡ δικαιοσύνη (Kyrios hē dikaiosynē) – meaning
"The Lord our righteousness"
English: The Lord Our Righteousness

SCRIPTURAL REFERENCE:

"In His days Judah will be saved, and Israel will dwell safely; and this is His name by which He will be called: 'The LORD Our Righteousness' (Jehovah Tsidkenu)."

Jeremiah 23:6

Jeremiah 33:16, Romans 3:22

DIVINE ENCOUNTERS

Hebrew: Jehovah Tsidkenu means "The Lord Our Righteousness." The word Tsidkenu (צִדְקֵנוּ) comes from Tsedek (צֶדֶק), meaning righteousness, justice, or rightness. This name signifies God's role as the source of righteousness for His people, emphasizing that true righteousness comes from Him alone.

Greek: In Greek, Kyrios hē dikaiosynē translates to "The Lord our righteousness," highlighting God's authority to declare His people righteous.

English: The phrase The Lord Our Righteousness conveys the understanding that God is both the standard of righteousness and the one who imparts righteousness to His people.

TIME OF AGE:

Biblical Context:

Jehovah Tsidkenu is revealed in the context of Jeremiah's prophecies concerning the coming Messiah and the restoration of Israel. During a time of moral decay and spiritual corruption, God promises a future king from David's line who will bring righteousness and justice. This name points to the hope of redemption through Christ, who embodies perfect righteousness and imparts it to believers.

Historical Context:

In ancient Israel, righteousness was a critical aspect of the covenant relationship between God and His people. The Israelites often strayed from God's commands, leading to judgment and exile. Jehovah Tsidkenu reminds them of God's faithfulness to provide a means of righteousness through His Messiah. This understanding would have been especially important during the Babylonian exile when the people felt abandoned and in need of restoration.

Theological Significance:

Jehovah Tsidkenu reveals that true righteousness is not something humans can achieve on their own but is a gift from God. This name emphasizes the necessity of a savior who would bear the sin of humanity and grant righteousness to those who believe. In the New Testament, this is fulfilled in Jesus Christ, who is described as our righteousness (Romans 3:22) and through whom believers are justified before God.

For Believers Today:

Understanding Jehovah Tsidkenu is foundational for Christian faith. It reassures believers that their righteousness is not based on their works but on their relationship with Christ, who imputes His righteousness to them. This name encourages humility, recognizing that we are dependent on God for our standing before Him. In times of failure or self-doubt, believers can remember that they are clothed in the righteousness of Christ, enabling them to approach God with confidence and live in accordance with His will.

DIVINE ENCOUNTERS

PRAYER

Jehovah Tsidkenu,

We come before You, acknowledging You as our Righteousness. Thank You for providing us with Your perfect righteousness through faith in Christ. Help us to understand that in our weakness, we can find strength and hope in You. May we reflect Your righteousness in our lives, living in a way that honors You and draws others to Your love. Teach us to rely on Your grace and to walk in Your truth daily. We are grateful for the gift of righteousness that transforms us and brings us into closer communion with You. In Jesus' name, we pray. Amen.

11
JEHOVAH SHAMMAH
(THE LORD IS THERE)

Hebrew: יְהוָה שָׁמָּה (YHWH Shammah)
Greek: Κύριος ἐκεῖ (Kyrios ekei) –
meaning "The Lord is there"
English: The Lord Is There

SCRIPTURAL REFERENCE:

"The perimeter of the city shall be eighteen thousand cubits. The name of the city from that day shall be, 'The LORD is there' (Jehovah Shammah)."

Ezekiel 48:35

Psalm 139:7-10, Matthew 28:20

Hebrew: Jehovah Shammah means "The Lord Is There." The term Shammah (שָׁמָּה) conveys the idea of presence, indicating that God is present among His people, providing comfort, protection, and guidance.

Greek: In Greek, Kyrios ekei translates to "The Lord is there," emphasizing God's continuous presence.

English: The phrase The Lord Is There encapsulates the promise of God's abiding presence with His people.

JEHOVAH SHAMMAH (THE LORD IS THERE)

TIME OF AGE:

Biblical Context:

Jehovah Shammah is revealed in the context of Ezekiel's vision of a restored Israel and the future temple. After a period of exile and destruction, God assures His people that He will once again dwell among them. The name signifies hope and restoration, emphasizing that God's presence is a central aspect of His relationship with His people.

Historical Context:

The concept of God's presence was vital for the Israelites, especially during the Babylonian exile. They longed for the return to Jerusalem and the restoration of the temple, which represented God's dwelling place among them. Naming the city Jehovah Shammah highlighted the reality that God's presence would be with

His people in their restored homeland, signifying comfort and divine assurance.

Theological Significance:

Jehovah Shammah reflects God's desire to be in relationship with His people. It reveals that God is not distant or detached but intimately involved in the lives of His people. This name foreshadows the incarnation of Christ, who is Immanuel, meaning "God with us" (Matthew 1:23). It assures believers that God's presence is always accessible, providing comfort in times of trouble and assurance of His love and guidance.

For Believers Today:

Jehovah Shammah encourages believers to recognize and appreciate the constant presence of God in their lives. Whether in moments of joy or in times of struggle, we can rest assured that God is with us. This name invites us to cultivate an awareness

JEHOVAH SHAMMAH (THE LORD IS THERE)

of God's presence, fostering a deeper relationship with Him through prayer, worship, and meditation on His Word. It reassures us that we are never alone; God is always near, offering support, guidance, and comfort in our daily lives.

DIVINE ENCOUNTERS

PRAYER

Jehovah Shammah,

Thank You for being our ever-present God. We are grateful that You are always with us, surrounding us with Your love and protection. In times of uncertainty and fear, remind us of Your abiding presence that brings peace and comfort to our hearts. Help us to trust in Your nearness and to draw strength from knowing that we are never alone. May we live in awareness of Your presence, sharing Your love and light with those around us. In Jesus' name, we pray. Amen.

12
EMMANUEL
(GOD WITH US)

Hebrew: עִמָּנוּ אֵל (Immanu El)
Greek: Ἐμμανουήλ (Emmanouēl) –
meaning "God with us"
English: God with Us

SCRIPTURAL REFERENCE:

"Therefore the Lord Himself will give you a sign: The virgin will conceive and give birth to a son, and will call Him Immanuel."

Isaiah 7:14

Matthew 1:23, John 1:14

Hebrew: Emmanuel means "God with us." The term Immanu (עִמָּנוּ) signifies "with us," while El (אֵל) refers to God. This name emphasizes God's promise to be present with His people, fulfilling His covenant and demonstrating His love and care.

Greek: The Greek form Emmanouēl carries the same meaning, affirming the presence of God in human form through Jesus Christ.

English: In English, God with Us conveys the profound truth of God's presence among humanity, especially in the person of Jesus.

EMMANUEL (GOD WITH US)

TIME OF AGE:

Biblical Context:

The prophecy of Emmanuel is first given in Isaiah during a time of political upheaval for Israel. God reassures His people that He is with them even in their struggles and fears. In the New Testament, this promise is fulfilled through the birth of Jesus, who embodies God's presence on earth, establishing a new covenant with humanity.

Historical Context:

The name Emmanuel was particularly significant for the Israelites during times of crisis, reminding them that God was not distant but actively involved in their lives. The promise of Emmanuel brought hope during the Assyrian threat and later during the Babylonian exile, signifying God's faithfulness to His people.

Theological Significance:

Emmanuel represents the incarnation of Christ—God taking on human form to dwell among us. This name encapsulates the essence of the Gospel: God loves humanity so deeply that He chose to be with us, experiencing our joys and sorrows, ultimately leading to redemption through His death and resurrection.

For Believers Today:

The name Emmanuel offers profound assurance that God is always present with us, guiding and comforting us through life's challenges. It encourages believers to invite God's presence into every aspect of their lives, knowing that we do not navigate our struggles alone. This awareness can transform our experiences, leading us to live in faith and confidence.

EMMANUEL (GOD WITH US)

PRAYER

Father Emmanuel,

Thank You for the gift of Emmanuel, for the assurance that You are always with us. In moments of doubt, fear, and uncertainty, remind us of Your unwavering presence. Help us to feel Your closeness and to trust in Your guidance. May we invite You into every part of our lives, knowing that with You by our side, we can face any challenge. Let Your presence fill us with peace, joy, and strength as we walk in faith. In Jesus' name, we pray. Amen.

13

YAHWEH YIREH
(THE LORD WILL PROVIDE)

Hebrew: יְהוָה יִרְאֶה (YHWH Yireh)
Greek: Κύριος ὁ ἐπισκοπῶν
(Kyrios ho episkopōn) – meaning
"The Lord who provides"
English: The Lord Will Provide

SCRIPTURAL REFERENCE:

"So Abraham called that place The LORD Will Provide (Yahweh Yireh). And to this day it is said, 'On the mountain of the LORD it will be provided.'"

Genesis 22:14

DIVINE ENCOUNTERS

Philippians 4:19, Matthew 6:31-33

Hebrew: Yahweh Yireh translates to "The Lord Will Provide." The word Yireh (יִרְאֶה) comes from the root ra'ah (רָאָה), which means "to see." This name emphasizes God's ability to foresee our needs and provide for them according to His perfect will and timing.

Greek: In Greek, Kyrios ho episkopōn translates to "The Lord who provides," underscoring God's active role in supplying what is necessary for His people.

English: The phrase The Lord Will Provide expresses the promise that God sees our needs and will meet them, often in ways we cannot foresee.

YAHWEH YIREH (THE LORD WILL PROVIDE)

TIME OF AGE:

Biblical Context:

The name Yahweh Yireh is revealed during the story of Abraham and Isaac, when God provides a ram as a substitute for Isaac during the sacrifice. This moment illustrates not only God's provision in a time of deep personal trial for Abraham but also foreshadows God's ultimate provision through Jesus Christ as the Lamb for humanity.

Historical Context:

For the ancient Israelites, this name would have been a powerful reminder of God's faithfulness and provision during their journey through the wilderness, as they relied on Him for sustenance and guidance. It reinforced their identity as a people who were dependent on God for all their needs.

Theological Significance:

Yahweh Yireh highlights God's character as a provider, revealing that He is attentive to our needs and desires to bless His people. This name encourages trust in God's goodness and faithfulness, reassuring us that He will provide for us spiritually, physically, and emotionally. It points to the ultimate provision of salvation through Christ, who meets our deepest need for redemption.

For Believers Today:

Yahweh Yireh reminds us to trust in God's provision in every aspect of our lives. Whether we are facing financial struggles, health issues, or relational challenges, we can rest assured that God sees our needs and is working on our behalf. This name encourages us to approach God with our requests, reminding us that He is faithful and able to provide for us abundantly according to His will.

YAHWEH YIREH (THE LORD WILL PROVIDE)

PRAYER

Gracious Yahweh Yireh,

Thank You for being Yahweh Yireh, the Lord who provides. Help us to trust in Your provision during times of uncertainty and need. When we feel overwhelmed or anxious about our circumstances, remind us that You see us and know our needs. Strengthen our faith as we wait for Your timing and provision. May we always remember to seek Your kingdom first, knowing that You will provide everything we need. In Jesus' name, we pray. Amen.

14
JEHOVAH ROHI
(THE LORD IS MY SHEPHERD)

Hebrew: יְהוָה רֹעִי (YHWH Rohi)
Greek: Κύριος ὁ ποιμήν μου (Kyrios ho poimēn mou) – meaning
"The Lord is my shepherd"
English: The Lord Is My Shepherd

SCRIPTURAL REFERENCE:

"The LORD is my shepherd; I shall not want."

Psalm 23:1

John 10:11-14, Ezekiel 34:11-16

Hebrew: Jehovah Rohi translates to "The Lord Is My Shepherd." The term Rohi (רֹעִי) is derived from the root ra'ah (רָאָה), which means "to feed" or "to tend." This name emphasizes God's care, guidance, and provision for His people, portraying Him as a loving shepherd who leads, protects, and nurtures.

Greek: The Greek translation Kyrios ho poimēn mou conveys the same meaning, highlighting the intimate relationship between God and His people as a shepherd to his flock.

English: In English, The Lord Is My Shepherd reflects the comforting and guiding presence of God in the lives of believers.

JEHOVAH ROHI (THE LORD IS MY SHEPHERD)

TIME OF AGE:

Biblical Context:

The name Jehovah Rohi is famously articulated in Psalm 23, a passage expressing deep trust in God's provision and care. David, a shepherd himself, uses this metaphor to convey his understanding of God as the ultimate shepherd who guides His people through life's challenges, providing them with comfort and security.

Historical Context:

In ancient Israel, shepherding was a common and significant occupation. Shepherds had a deep responsibility for their flocks, often risking their lives to protect them from predators. This cultural backdrop enriches the understanding of God's role as a protector and guide, especially for a people who faced various threats and challenges.

Theological Significance:

Jehovah Rohi reveals God's desire to be intimately involved in the lives of His people, offering direction, comfort, and protection. This name is fulfilled in Jesus Christ, who describes Himself as the Good Shepherd in John 10, highlighting His sacrificial love for His sheep. It assures believers that they are valued and cared for by God, who desires to lead them on the right path.

For Believers Today:

Understanding Jehovah Rohi invites believers to rely on God for guidance and care in their daily lives. Just as a shepherd leads his sheep to green pastures and still waters, God provides peace and nourishment for our souls. In times of confusion, fear, or uncertainty, we can rest in the knowledge that our Shepherd is always near, guiding us and protecting us. This name encourages us to cultivate a

JEHOVAH ROHI (THE LORD IS MY SHEPHERD)

personal relationship with God, trusting in His wisdom and care as we navigate life's challenges.

DIVINE ENCOUNTERS

PRAYER

Dear Shepherd of our souls,

Thank You for being Jehovah Rohi, the Lord who guides and cares for us. Help us to trust in Your leadership as we navigate the complexities of life. When we feel lost or anxious, remind us that You are with us, providing comfort and direction. May we always find rest in Your presence and rely on Your wisdom as our guide. Help us to follow You closely and to share Your love and care with others as we walk in faith. In Jesus' name, we pray. Amen.

15

EL ROI
(THE GOD WHO SEES)

Hebrew: אֵל רֳאִי (El Roi)
Greek: Θεὸς ὁ ὁρῶν (Theos ho horōn) –
meaning "God who sees"
English: The God Who Sees

SCRIPTURAL REFERENCE:

"So she called the name of the LORD who spoke to her, 'You are a God of seeing' (El Roi), for she said, 'Truly here I have seen Him who looks after me.'"

Genesis 16:13

Psalm 33:18, Proverbs 15:3

Hebrew: El Roi translates to "The God Who Sees." The term Roi (רֹאִי) comes from the root ra'ah (רָאָה), meaning "to see." This name emphasizes God's awareness of our circumstances, struggles, and needs, affirming that He is attentive to our lives.

Greek: In Greek, Theos ho horōn conveys the same meaning, underscoring God's omniscience and care for His creation.

English: The phrase The God Who Sees captures the essence of God's active presence and involvement in our lives.

EL ROI (THE GOD WHO SEES)

TIME OF AGE:

Biblical Context:

El Roi is revealed to Hagar, the servant of Sarah, when she flees into the wilderness after being mistreated. In her despair, God encounters her and assures her that He sees her plight and cares for her and her son Ishmael. This moment highlights God's compassion and attentiveness to those who are marginalized and in need.

Historical Context:

Hagar's experience illustrates the broader theme of God's concern for the vulnerable and oppressed. In ancient societies, those in positions of power often overlooked the needs of the weak, but El Roi stands as a testament to God's justice and care for all people, especially those in distress.

Theological Significance:

El Roi reveals that God is not only aware of our circumstances but is also actively involved in our lives. It reassures believers that they are never unseen or forgotten by God, no matter how dire their situation may seem. This name emphasizes God's loving nature and His desire to intervene in our lives for our good.

For Believers Today:

Understanding El Roi encourages believers to approach God with their concerns, knowing that He sees and cares for them. In moments of loneliness, despair, or uncertainty, we can find comfort in the truth that God is aware of our struggles and is working on our behalf. This name invites us to reflect on our own attentiveness to the needs of others, encouraging us to embody God's compassion and care in our relationships and communities.

EL ROI (THE GOD WHO SEES)

PRAYER

Gracious El Roi,

Thank You for being the God who sees us in our struggles and joys. We are grateful that You know our hearts, our fears, and our hopes. Help us to trust in Your awareness and care, especially in times when we feel overlooked or alone. May we find comfort in knowing that we are never hidden from Your sight. Open our eyes to see those around us who are in need, that we might reflect Your love and compassion in their lives. In Jesus' name, we pray. Amen.

16
JEHOVAH MEKODDISHKEM
(THE LORD WHO SANCTIFIES YOU)

Hebrew: יְהוָה מְקַדִּשְׁכֶם (YHWH Mekoddishkem)
Greek: Κύριος ὁ ἁγιάζων ὑμᾶς (Kyrios ho hagiadzōn humas) – meaning "The Lord who sanctifies you"
English: The Lord Who Sanctifies You

SCRIPTURAL REFERENCE:

"You are to speak to the people of Israel and say, 'You shall keep My Sabbaths, for this is a sign between Me and you throughout your generations, that you may know that I, the LORD, who sanctifies

you (Jehovah Mekoddishkem).'"

Exodus 31:13

Leviticus 20:8, 1 Thessalonians 5:23

Hebrew: Jehovah Mekoddishkem translates to "The Lord Who Sanctifies You." The term Mekoddishkem (מְקַדִּשְׁכֶם) comes from the root qadash (קָדַשׁ), meaning "to sanctify" or "to set apart." This name emphasizes God's role in making His people holy and set apart for His purposes.

Greek: The Greek translation Kyrios ho hagiadzōn humas highlights the action of sanctification, emphasizing that God actively purifies and prepares His people.

English: The Lord Who Sanctifies You signifies God's commitment to transforming His people into vessels of His holiness and righteousness.

TIME OF AGE:

Biblical Context:

The name Jehovah Mekoddishkem is revealed in the context of God's covenant with Israel, emphasizing the importance of obedience to His commands, particularly the Sabbath. This name assures the Israelites that their sanctification is rooted in their relationship with God and their adherence to His laws.

Historical Context:

In ancient Israel, sanctification was essential for the people to live in a way that honored God. Observing the Sabbath and following God's commandments were practices that set Israel apart from other nations, highlighting their unique relationship with God. This name reinforces the idea that holiness is not achieved through human effort alone but through God's transformative power.

Theological Significance:

Jehovah Mekoddishkem reveals God's desire for His people to be holy, reflecting His character. This sanctification is an ongoing process, empowering believers to live according to God's will. It points to the New Testament reality of being sanctified through the work of Christ, who cleanses us from sin and sets us apart for His service.

For Believers Today:

Understanding Jehovah Mekoddishkem encourages believers to embrace their identity as sanctified people, called to live in accordance with God's purposes. This name invites us to seek God's guidance in our lives, allowing Him to transform our hearts and minds. It calls us to engage in practices that promote holiness, such as prayer, studying Scripture, and engaging in community with other believers.

PRAYER

Holy Jehovah Mekoddishkem,

Thank You for being the Lord who sanctifies us and sets us apart for Your purposes. We are grateful for Your work in our lives, transforming us to reflect Your holiness and love. Help us to live in a way that honors You, seeking Your guidance and strength in every situation. May we be open to Your refining work, allowing You to shape us into the people You have called us to be. In Jesus' name, we pray. Amen.

17
EL OLAM
(THE EVERLASTING GOD)

Hebrew: אֵל עוֹלָם (El Olam)
Greek: Θεὸς ὁ αἰώνιος (Theos ho aiōnios)
– meaning "God the everlasting"
English: The Everlasting God

SCRIPTURAL REFERENCE:

"Abraham planted a tamarisk tree in Beersheba, and there he called on the name of the LORD, the Everlasting God (El Olam)."
Genesis 21:33

Isaiah 40:28, Psalm 90:1-2

Hebrew: El Olam translates to "The Everlasting God." The term Olam (עוֹלָם) refers to eternity or an age without end, signifying God's timeless nature and eternal existence. This name emphasizes that God is not bound by time and His purposes endure forever.

Greek: In Greek, Theos ho aiōnios conveys the concept of eternity, affirming God's unchanging and everlasting nature. English: The phrase The Everlasting God captures the essence of God's infinite nature, highlighting His eternal faithfulness and sovereignty.

EL OLAM (THE EVERLASTING GOD)

TIME OF AGE:

Biblical Context:

The name El Olam is introduced in the context of Abraham's covenant with God, reinforcing the idea that God's promises are not temporary but everlasting. This name assures believers that God's character and promises remain steadfast throughout all generations.

Historical Context:

In ancient Near Eastern culture, the concept of eternity was often linked to the gods of various peoples. However, El Olam sets God apart as the only true everlasting deity, whose existence transcends all time and history. It reassures the faithful that, unlike worldly powers and deities, God is eternal and unchanging. Theological Significance: El Olam reveals God's nature as the eternal Creator, underscoring His omnipotence and omniscience. This name is a reminder that God's plans and purposes will prevail regardless of human circumstances. It encourages believers to trust in His eternal promises and to find hope in His everlasting presence.

For Believers Today:

Understanding El Olam encourages believers to cultivate a perspective that transcends the temporary challenges of life. Recognizing God as the Everlasting God invites us to trust in His eternal nature and the permanence of His promises. In a world marked by change and uncertainty, we can find peace and assurance in the fact that God is constant and faithful.

EL OLAM (THE EVERLASTING GOD)

PRAYER

Eternal El Olam,

Thank You for being the Everlasting God, who reigns beyond time and circumstance. We are grateful for Your unchanging nature and the eternal promises You have made to us. Help us to place our trust in Your everlasting faithfulness, especially in times of uncertainty or doubt. May we find hope in Your eternal presence and live with a perspective that reflects Your timeless truth. In Jesus' name, we pray. Amen.

18

JEHOVAH SABAOTH
(THE LORD OF HOSTS)

Hebrew: יְהוָה צְבָאוֹת (YHWH Sabaoth)
Greek: Κύριος τῶν δυνάμεων (Kyrios tōn dunameōn) – meaning
"The Lord of powers"
English: The Lord of Hosts

SCRIPTURAL REFERENCE:

"Now this man used to go up year by year from his city to worship and to sacrifice to the LORD of hosts (Jehovah Sabaoth) at Shiloh."

Isaiah 6:3, Psalm 46:7

Hebrew: Jehovah Sabaoth translates to "The Lord of Hosts." The term Sabaoth (צְבָאוֹת) refers to "hosts" or "armies," emphasizing God's authority over the heavenly hosts and earthly powers. This name highlights God's sovereignty and power in both spiritual and earthly realms.

Greek: In Greek, Kyrios tōn dunameōn reflects the same meaning, affirming God's dominion over all forces and powers.

English: The Lord of Hosts conveys the idea that God is the supreme commander over all heavenly beings and earthly armies, highlighting His unmatched authority.

JEHOVAH SABAOTH (THE LORD OF HOSTS)

TIME OF AGE:

Biblical Context:

The name Jehovah Sabaoth appears frequently in the Old Testament, particularly in the context of Israel's battles and God's protection of His people. It assures them that God is their defender and that He fights on their behalf. This name encapsulates the assurance of God's presence with His people, especially in times of conflict or struggle.

Historical Context:

In ancient Israel, military strength was vital for survival. The assurance that God is the Lord of Hosts would have given the Israelites confidence in their battles, reinforcing their belief that victory comes from divine intervention rather than mere human effort. Theological Significance:

Jehovah Sabaoth reveals God's power and authority over all creation. It emphasizes His role as protector and warrior for His people. This name reassures believers that they are not alone in their struggles; God is actively engaged in their lives and fights for their well-being.

For Believers Today:

Understanding Jehovah Sabaoth encourages believers to recognize that God is always present and fighting for them in spiritual and physical battles. In times of fear or uncertainty, they can find strength and courage in the knowledge that God, as the Lord of Hosts, is on their side. This name calls believers to trust in God's power and to seek His guidance and strength in every circumstance.

JEHOVAH SABAOTH (THE LORD OF HOSTS)

PRAYER

Mighty Jehovah Sabaoth

Thank You for being the Lord of Hosts, who fights for us and protects us. We are grateful for Your presence and power in our lives, especially during times of struggle or conflict. Help us to trust in Your strength and to find peace in the knowledge that You are with us. May we always turn to You in prayer, seeking Your guidance and support as we navigate the battles of life. Empower us to stand firm in faith, knowing that with You on our side, we can overcome any obstacle. In Jesus' name, we pray. Amen.

19
THE ROCK

Hebrew: הַצּוּר (HaTsur)
Greek: ὁ πέτρος (ho petros) –
meaning "the rock"
English: The Rock

SCRIPTURAL REFERENCE:

"The Rock (HaTsur), His work is perfect, for all His ways are justice. A God of faithfulness and without iniquity, just and upright is He."

Deuteronomy 32:4

Psalm 18:2, Matthew 16:18

Hebrew: The Rock (HaTsur) symbolizes stability, strength, and security. In the Old Testament, it refers to God as a refuge and a source of protection for His people, emphasizing His unchanging and solid nature.

Greek: The Greek word ho petros conveys the same meaning, reinforcing the idea of a firm foundation and reliable support.

English: The Rock signifies God's enduring strength and reliability, serving as a metaphor for His protection and faithfulness.

THE ROCK

TIME OF AGE:

Biblical Context:

The name The Rock is used throughout Scripture to portray God's character as a steadfast protector. In Deuteronomy, Moses refers to God as The Rock to emphasize His reliability and the faithfulness of His covenant with Israel. This imagery continues into the New Testament, where Jesus refers to Peter as a rock, symbolizing the foundation of the Church built upon faith in Him.

Historical Context:

In ancient Near Eastern cultures, rocky terrain was often seen as a source of strength and security. The metaphor of a rock would resonate deeply with people accustomed to the dangers of the wilderness and the threats from enemies. God being depicted as The Rock reassured the Israelites of His protection and unwavering support in a tumultuous world.

Theological Significance:

The Rock underscores God's unchanging nature and His role as a refuge for His people. It emphasizes that when life's storms arise, God is a safe place to find shelter and strength. This name reminds believers of the stability found in their relationship with God and the assurance that He is always present.

For Believers Today:

Understanding The Rock encourages believers to seek refuge in God during challenging times. When facing difficulties, they can find comfort in knowing that God is their firm foundation and source of strength. This name invites believers to deepen their trust in God's faithfulness, reminding them to anchor their lives in His unchanging nature rather than the shifting sands of circumstance.

DIVINE ENCOUNTERS

PRAYER

Rock of Ages,

Thank You for being our solid foundation and steadfast refuge. We are grateful for Your strength and reliability in every season of life. Help us to turn to You when we face storms and uncertainties, trusting that You will provide the shelter and security we need. May we stand firm in our faith, knowing that our lives are anchored in You. Teach us to share Your strength with others who may be struggling, reflecting Your love and stability in their lives. In Jesus' name, we pray. Amen.

20
THE WORD

Hebrew: דָּבָר (Davar)
Greek: Λόγος (Logos) – meaning "Word"
English: The Word

SCRIPTURAL REFERENCE:

"In the beginning was the Word (Logos), and the Word was with God, and the Word was God."

John 1:1

Revelation 19:13, Psalm 119:105

Hebrew: Davar means "word" or "thing," and in the biblical context, it often refers to God's message, commandments, and creative power. It emphasizes the authority and impact of God's spoken word in creation and revelation.

Greek: The term Logos carries profound significance in the New Testament, particularly in the writings of John. It encapsulates the idea of Jesus as the divine expression of God, embodying truth, life, and revelation to humanity.

English: The Word signifies Jesus Christ, affirming His role as the communication of God's will, wisdom, and presence in the world.

THE WORD

TIME OF AGE:

Biblical Context:

In the prologue of John's Gospel, The Word establishes the pre-existence of Christ and His divine nature. It emphasizes that Jesus is not just a messenger but is, in fact, God Himself. This name connects the Old Testament understanding of God's spoken word with the New Testament revelation of Jesus as the living Word.

Historical Context:

In the ancient world, the concept of the Logos was significant in both Jewish and Hellenistic thought. For Jews, the Word of God was powerful and transformative, while in Hellenistic philosophy, the Logos represented reason and order in the universe. John's use of the term bridges these understandings, presenting Jesus as the ultimate revelation of God's nature and purpose.

Theological Significance:

The Word reveals the intimate relationship between God and humanity through Jesus. It underscores the belief that through Christ, believers can know God, experience His grace, and receive His truth. This name affirms the centrality of Scripture in the life of believers, as the Word guides and nourishes their faith.

For Believers Today:

Understanding The Word encourages believers to engage deeply with Scripture, recognizing it as God's communication to them. It invites them to read, meditate on, and apply God's Word in their lives, allowing it to shape their thoughts, actions, and relationship with Him. This name also calls believers to proclaim the truth of Jesus, the living Word, in their communities and to share the message of hope and salvation.

THE WORD

PRAYER

Heavenly Father,

Thank You for being The Word, who brings life, truth, and revelation into our lives. We are grateful for the gift of Scripture and the way it guides us in our journey of faith. Help us to dive deeply into Your Word, allowing it to transform our hearts and minds. May we recognize Jesus as the living Word and share His love and truth with others. Equip us to be messengers of Your hope in a world that desperately needs Your light. In Jesus' name, we pray. Amen.

21
THE HOLY ONE OF ISRAEL

Hebrew: קָדוֹשׁ יִשְׂרָאֵל (Kedosh Yisrael)
Greek: ὁ ἅγιος Ἰσραὴλ (ho hagios Israēl)
– meaning "the Holy One of Israel"
English: The Holy One of Israel

SCRIPTURAL REFERENCE:

"For I am the LORD your God, the Holy One of Israel, your Savior."

Isaiah 43:3

Psalm 30:4, Isaiah 12:6

Hebrew: Kedosh Yisrael translates to "The Holy One of Israel." The term Kedosh (קָדוֹשׁ) means "holy," signifying purity, separateness, and divine nature. This name emphasizes God's moral perfection and His unique relationship with the nation of Israel, chosen for His purpose and covenant.

Greek: In Greek, ho hagios Israēl reiterates the holiness of God, underscoring His distinction from all creation and His purity.

English: The Holy One of Israel signifies God's sovereignty, holiness, and role as the Savior for His people.

THE HOLY ONE OF ISRAEL

TIME OF AGE:

Biblical Context:

The name The Holy One of Israel is frequently used in the prophetic books, particularly Isaiah, to remind Israel of God's holiness and His commitment to their salvation. It serves as both a warning against sin and an assurance of redemption, emphasizing that despite their failings, God remains holy and faithful to His promises.

Historical Context:

In ancient Israel, the holiness of God was a foundational concept, influencing their worship practices and understanding of His nature. God's designation as "The Holy One of Israel" reinforces the idea that He is set apart from all nations and idols, commanding the reverence and devotion of His people.

Theological Significance:

The Holy One of Israel highlights the dual aspects of God's nature: His holiness and His grace. It reminds believers that while God is completely pure and just, He is also intimately involved in the lives of His people, offering salvation and guidance. This name encourages a response of worship and reverence.

For Believers Today:

Understanding The Holy One of Israel invites believers to reflect on God's holiness and their own call to holiness. It encourages them to pursue a relationship with God that acknowledges His purity and grace. This name serves as a reminder that God desires His people to live in a way that honors His holiness, and it prompts believers to share His holiness with others.

THE HOLY ONE OF ISRAEL

PRAYER

Holy One of Israel,

Thank You for being our Savior and the embodiment of holiness. We are grateful for Your commitment to us, even when we fall short. Help us to recognize Your holiness in our lives and inspire us to pursue a life that reflects Your purity and love. May we honor You in our thoughts, actions, and relationships, and may we share Your truth and grace with those around us. In Jesus' name, we pray. Amen.

22

THE LION OF THE TRIBE OF JUDAH

Hebrew: אַרְיֵה מִשֵּׁבֶט יְהוּדָה
(Ari miShevet Yehudah)
Greek: ὁ λέων ἐκ τῆς φυλῆς Ἰούδα (ho leōn ek tēs phylēs Iouda) – meaning "the lion from the tribe of Judah"
English: The Lion of the Tribe of Judah

SCRIPTURAL REFERENCE:

"And one of the elders said to me, 'Weep no more; behold, the Lion of the tribe of Judah, the Root of David, has conquered, so that he can open the scroll and its seven seals.'"

Revelation 5:5

Genesis 49:9, Hebrews 7:14

Hebrew: Ari miShevet Yehudah refers to the Lion as a symbol of strength, power, and leadership. The tribe of Judah was one of the most prominent tribes of Israel, and the lion symbolizes both royalty and ferocity in battle. This name signifies Jesus' kingship and authority over His people.

Greek: The term ho leōn ek tēs phylēs Iouda also captures the strength and majesty associated with the lion, emphasizing Jesus' rightful place as the powerful Messiah who fulfills God's promises.

English: The Lion of the Tribe of Judah emphasizes Jesus' identity as the victorious King and Savior, highlighting His authority over sin, death, and the powers of darkness.

TIME OF AGE:

Biblical Context:

The imagery of the Lion of Judah is deeply rooted in the Old Testament, particularly in Jacob's blessing of his sons in Genesis, where Judah is described as a lion's cub. This foreshadows the royal lineage that would lead to the Messiah. In Revelation, the title emphasizes Jesus' triumph and sovereignty as the ultimate King, who overcomes the enemy and restores God's Kingdom.

Historical Context:

In ancient Israel, the lion was a powerful symbol of strength and courage, representing the ideals of leadership and kingship. Judah was seen as a tribe of warriors, and the lion symbolizes the pride and strength of this tribe, which would produce the Davidic line from which Jesus descends.

Theological Significance:

The Lion of the Tribe of Judah illustrates the dual nature of Christ as both the suffering servant and the conquering King. It signifies His power to redeem and to reign, reassuring believers that He has the authority to overcome any opposition they may face.

For Believers Today:

Understanding The Lion of the Tribe of Judah encourages believers to have confidence in Christ's victory over sin and death. It reassures them of His power and authority in their lives, inviting them to trust in His ability to protect and lead them. This name inspires believers to stand firm in their faith, knowing that they serve a powerful and victorious Savior.

PRAYER

Lion of the Tribe of Judah,

Thank You for being our mighty King and conqueror. We are grateful for Your victory over sin and death, and for the strength You provide in our lives. Help us to stand firm in faith, trusting in Your power and authority as we navigate the challenges of life. May we boldly proclaim Your victory to others and live in a way that reflects Your strength and courage. In Jesus' name, we pray. Amen.

23
THE ANCIENT OF DAYS

Hebrew: עַתִּיק יוֹמִין (Atiq Yomin)
Greek: ὁ Παλαιὸς τῶν ἡμερῶν (ho Palaios tōn hēmerōn) – meaning "the Ancient of Days"
English: The Ancient of Days

SCRIPTURAL REFERENCE:

"As I looked, thrones were placed, and the Ancient of Days took his seat; his clothing was white as snow, and the hair of his head like pure wool; his throne was fiery flames; its wheels were burning fire."

Daniel 7:9

Daniel 7:13-14, Psalm 90:2

Hebrew: Atiq Yomin translates to "the Ancient of Days," indicating God's eternal nature and sovereignty over time. The title emphasizes His wisdom and authority as the everlasting ruler who exists beyond the limitations of human understanding and temporal existence.

Greek: The term ho Palaios tōn hēmerōn conveys similar meanings of timelessness and the divine nature of God, reinforcing His position as the ultimate authority.

English: The Ancient of Days signifies God's eternal existence, highlighting His sovereignty, wisdom, and the idea that He is unaffected by time.

TIME OF AGE:

Biblical Context:

The title The Ancient of Days is used in the context of Daniel's vision of the end times, where God is portrayed as a judge who will execute justice. This emphasizes His eternal authority and the certainty of His sovereign rule, even as earthly powers rise and fall.

Historical Context:

In ancient Near Eastern cultures, the concept of an eternal deity was common, and the Ancient of Days represents the ultimate authority and wisdom that surpasses all creation. This title reassures believers of God's enduring presence and His ultimate control over history.

Theological Significance:

The Ancient of Days emphasizes God's

immutability and sovereignty. It reassures believers that God is in control of time and history, encouraging them to trust in His plan and purpose. This name reflects the belief that while human circumstances may change, God remains the same.

For Believers Today:

Understanding The Ancient of Days invites believers to reflect on God's eternal nature and sovereignty. It encourages them to find peace in knowing that God is not bound by time and that He has a plan for their lives. This name inspires believers to trust in God's timing and to seek His wisdom in their decisions.

THE ANCIENT OF DAYS

PRAYER

Ancient of Days,

Thank You for being eternal and unchanging in a world that constantly shifts. We are grateful for Your sovereignty and wisdom, knowing that You hold all of history in Your hands. Help us to trust in Your perfect timing and guidance as we navigate life's challenges. May we find peace in Your presence and share the assurance of Your eternal love with those around us. In Jesus' name, we pray. Amen.

24
EHYEH ASHER EHYEH

Hebrew: אֶהְיֶה אֲשֶׁר אֶהְיֶה
(Ehyeh Asher Ehyeh)
Greek: ἐγώ εἰμι ὁ ὤν (egō eimi ho ōn) –
meaning "I AM who I AM"
English: I AM WHO I AM

SCRIPTURAL REFERENCE:

"God said to Moses, 'I AM WHO I AM.' And he said, 'Say this to the people of Israel: 'I AM has sent me to you.'"

Exodus 3:14

John 8:58, Revelation 1:8

Hebrew: Ehyeh Asher Ehyeh can be translated as "I AM who I AM," indicating God's self-existence, eternal nature, and unchanging character. This name signifies that God is not defined by anything outside Himself and exists independently of time, space, or circumstances.

Greek: The Greek translation, egō eimi ho ōn, underscores the essence of being and existence. It emphasizes that God is the ultimate reality and the source of all being.

English: I AM WHO I AM signifies God's eternal presence, affirming that He is all-sufficient and capable of fulfilling His promises.

EHYEH ASHER EHYEH

TIME OF AGE:

Biblical Context:

This name is revealed to Moses at the burning bush when God commissions him to lead the Israelites out of Egypt. It signifies God's authority and the assurance that He is with His people, emphasizing His power to act and intervene in history.

Historical Context:

In the context of ancient Near Eastern religions, the declaration of God's name in this way emphasizes His uniqueness and transcendence. Unlike the gods of surrounding cultures, who were often tied to specific places or times, the God of Israel is the ultimate reality, existing outside of human constraints.

Theological Significance:

Ehyeh Asher Ehyeh reflects God's

sovereignty and faithfulness. It assures believers of His unchanging nature and presence, encouraging them to trust in Him regardless of their circumstances. This name highlights that God is always present and available to His people.

For Believers Today:

Understanding Ehyeh Asher Ehyeh invites believers to recognize God's eternal nature and reliability. It encourages them to lean on God in times of uncertainty, knowing that He is always with them and will fulfill His promises. This name inspires believers to approach God with reverence, knowing they serve the great "I AM."

PRAYER

Ehyeh Asher Ehyeh,

Thank You for revealing Yourself as the great "I AM." We are grateful for Your eternal presence and unchanging nature, knowing that You are always with us. Help us to trust in Your promises and to find strength in Your sufficiency. May we live in a way that reflects Your holiness and share Your love with those around us. In Jesus' name, we pray. Amen.

CONCLUSION

As we reflect on the names of the Lord, we discover a profound tapestry of His character and nature that reveals His eternal presence, love, and sovereignty in our lives. Each name carries deep significance, reflecting God's promises, His unwavering faithfulness, and His intimate relationship with humanity. From El Shaddai, the All-Sufficient One, to Ehyeh Asher Ehyeh, the Great I AM, we are reminded that God is our provider, protector, healer, and Savior.

These names encourage us to trust in Him during times of uncertainty and to draw near to Him in worship and prayer. As we recognize His attributes, we find comfort, strength, and hope for our journey. We are invited to share His love and truth with others, embodying His light in a world that often feels dark.

May our understanding of these divine names transform our hearts, deepen our faith, and inspire us to live boldly for Him.

CONCLUSION

FINAL PRAYER

Heavenly Father,

As we conclude this journey through the names of the Lord, we thank You for the rich revelation of who You are. Your names remind us of Your greatness, love, and unwavering faithfulness. Help us to internalize these truths and to live in a way that reflects Your character in our daily lives.

May we find strength in Your names when we face challenges, comfort in Your presence when we are weary, and hope in Your promises as we navigate life's uncertainties. Empower us to share Your love with those around us, shining brightly as Your representatives in this world.

Thank You for being our God, our guide, and our friend. We trust in You and surrender our hearts to Your will. In the mighty name of Jesus, we pray. Amen.

www.ingramcontent.com/pod-product-compliance
Lightning Source LLC
Chambersburg PA
CBHW072016120225
21840CB00004B/71